Animal Coats

Written by Jo Windsor

The duck has feathers.

The bird has feathers.

The hen has feathers.

The sheep has wool.

The cat has fur.

The rabbit has fur.

The fish has scales.

The snake has scales.

The porcupine has spikes.

The hedgehog has spikes.

The horse has hair.

The girl has hair.

Index

▬▬▬ Guide Notes

Title: Animal Coats
Stage: Emergent – Magenta

Genre: Nonfiction (Expository)
Approach: Guided Reading
Processes: Thinking Critically, Exploring Language, Processing Information
Written and Visual Focus: Photographs (static images), Illustrations, Index
Word Count: 48

READING THE TEXT

Tell the children that this book is about what covers some animals' bodies.
Talk to them about what is on the front cover. Read the title and the author.
Focus the children's attention on the index and talk about the animals that are in this book.
"Walk" through the book, focusing on the photographs and talk about the different coats the animals have.
Read the text together.

THINKING CRITICALLY
(sample questions)
- How do the different coverings help the animals?
- Which animals' coats in this book are soft, hard, spiky?

EXPLORING LANGUAGE
(ideas for selection)

Terminology
Title, cover, author, photographs, illustrations

Vocabulary
Interest words: feathers, wool, fur, scales, spikes, hair
High-frequency words: the, has